American Landmarks

The McCormick Apartments-Andrew Mellon
Building (1915–17), now the headquarters of
the National Trust for Historic Preservation.

Main entrance to Woodlawn Plantation near Mount Vernon, Va. (Marler Photo)

American Landmarks

HISTORIC PROPERTIES
OF THE NATIONAL TRUST FOR
HISTORIC PRESERVATION

YORK GRAPHIC SERVICES, INC. • YORK, PENNSYLVANIA

Christmas 1980

*The National Trust for Historic Preservation,
chartered by Congress in 1949, is the only national
private, nonprofit organization with the
responsibility to encourage public participation in
the preservation of sites, buildings and objects
significant in American history and culture. Support
is provided by membership dues, endowment funds,
contributions and matching grants from federal
agencies, including the U.S. Department of the
Interior, Heritage Conservation and Recreation
Service, under provisions of the National Historic
Preservation Act of 1966.*

*For information on membership, services or
publications, write or call: National Trust for Historic
Preservation, 1785 Massachusetts Avenue, N.W.,
Washington, D.C. 20036 (202) 673-4000.*

*This book was edited by Diane Maddex, senior
editor for preservation books, The Preservation Press.*

*Property essays were prepared by Robert Mawson,
museum programs assistant, Office of Historic
Properties, under the direction of Theodore A. Sande,
vice president, Office of Historic Properties, National
Trust for Historic Preservation. The assistance of the
following is gratefully acknowledged for research and
publications on which several essays are based:
Frederick D. Nichols, FAIA, for Belle Grove; Donald G.
Kalec, Thomas A. Heinz and the Restoration
Committee of the Frank Lloyd Wright Home and
Studio Foundation, for the Frank Lloyd Wright Home
and Studio; and Friends of Filoli, for Filoli.
Information on other National Trust properties
included here has been published previously by the
National Trust.*

Foreword

What difference does it make if a historic property is lost? A great deal of difference, I think.

First let me define just what makes a property "historic." It is not strictly age. This quality must be linked to cultural significance, something special from our past.

That something may be association with an important person, event or era, or perhaps a superior artistic or technical achievement. These are qualities worth our bother.

Such places are tangible reminders of what our ancestors have done, either knowingly or inadvertently, to shape our civilization. They tell us what we as a people have become and provide reference points of cultural excellence against which each generation can measure itself and in turn be measured. The loss of these reminders is like losing our memory.

Since its establishment in 1949, the National Trust for Historic Preservation has helped organizations and individuals to preserve this country's historic properties through advisory services, educational programs, publications and financial aid. It also owns and administers numerous historic properties itself and oversees an active program to develop innovative strategies for saving and reusing other such sites across the country. Chartered by Congress to encourage public participation in historic preservation, the National Trust (a private, nonprofit organization) is authorized to receive donations of sites, buildings and objects significant in American history and culture, and to preserve and administer them for public benefit. The National Trust now operates directly eight historic museums and has five co-stewardship properties. With the exception of those not regularly opened, these properties are presented on the following pages.

National Trust historic museums are properties of the highest caliber that illustrate and commemorate the history, culture or architecture of the United States. They are maintained by the National Trust as museums and community preservation centers where interpretive programs and activities emphasize preservation in general and the area surrounding the property in particular. Co-stewardship properties of the National Trust are operated under cooperative agreements with local preservation and related associations.

The breadth and diversity of American life are reflected in the historic properties of the National Trust. While each property represents a different aspect of the nation's architectural and historical development, each is also symbolic of the wide-ranging preservation efforts of the National Trust.

The National Trust's own headquarters is in an early 20th-century apartment building (1915–17), a National Historic Landmark in Washington, D.C., that has served as an office building since the late 1930s and was rehabilitated for National Trust use in 1979.

As community preservation centers, National Trust properties provide a link between the individuals and groups in their locales and the National Trust headquarters and its six regional offices across the nation. Because of their unique characters and diversity, the properties are used by the National Trust to supplement its services and to serve as laboratories for developing new preservation programs and techniques useful to preservationists nationwide.

Although these sites form the core of the National Trust historic properties program, our more recent emphasis is on assisting the preservation of significant historic properties by methods that do not involve acquisition and operation on a continuing basis by the National Trust. In this regard, the National Trust provides a stewardship role by retaining preservation easements on two dozen selected properties to assure their continued safe existence without National Trust ownership.

The National Trust also fulfills its charter by using a wide range of preservation methods and real estate techniques to carry out demonstration projects to save historic properties. In addition to accepting and encouraging preservation easements, the National Trust employs options and leases; resells asset properties with protective covenants; initiates feasibility studies and research projects; and administers a Restoration Workshop, which has its headquarters at Lyndhurst. Under its Endangered Properties Program, the National Trust maintains an inventory of nationally significant properties threatened by demolition, alteration or neglect and provides funding to save these endangered landmarks.

A balanced approach is the only sensible solution to saving historic properties. We have to fit the use of a historic property to its physical limitations and recognize its distinctive features. We must have the good sense and humility to understand the basic meaning of each place and to listen to what it tells us—and these are not always easy things to achieve.

Thus, to care for these places we must first understand them, and then we must discover how best to conserve these irreplaceable parts of our cultural heritage, these American landmarks, so that they may be shared with the public for whom we hold them in trust.

THEODORE A. SANDE
Vice President, Office of Historic Properties
National Trust for Historic Preservation

American Landmarks

The main house at Chesterwood on the left
(1900–01) with Daniel Chester French's studio
at right (1898). (Russell C. Hamilton)

Interior of the studio, with several versions of
French's "Seated Lincoln" (1911–22), "Andromeda"
(1929–31), other works and the
sculptor's tools. (Russell C. Hamilton)

Chesterwood

"I live here six months of the year—in heaven," sculptor Daniel Chester French once remarked to a visitor to his summer home. "The other six months of the year I live, well—in New York."

The idyllic setting to which French was referring was Chesterwood, the studio and summer residence near Stockbridge in the Berkshire Hills of Massachusetts where he worked for more than three decades. Today a historic house museum, Chesterwood is filled with sketches, plaster casts and bronze models of French's sculpture.

French discovered the setting on a carriage trip with his wife through the Housatonic River Valley in 1896. Looking for a summer home, the couple was shown the Marshall Warner farm. The view from the property of the Housatonic River and Monument Mountain beyond was "beautiful and soul-satisfying." French purchased the farm and began construction of a summer studio in 1898. The architect was his friend Henry Bacon (1866–1924), who later designed the Lincoln Memorial in Washington, D.C. It was in this studio that French completed many of his most famous works, including the "Seated Lincoln" for the Lincoln Memorial, dedicated in 1922.

French had definite requirements for his summer studio, requirements fulfilled by Bacon's design. Its work area is a 23-foot-high stucco and frame room. A high peaked ceiling with a large north skylight allowed ample space and light for the sculptor's work. Adjacent to the work area is a small room for casting plaster models. The entrance to the studio building is a living area with piano, fireplace and library where French rested and entertained his frequent guests. Doors from this reception area lead to a small terraced garden with a fountain designed by Bacon and embellished by French. Opposite the entrance is a piazza with a view of Monument Mountain.

The studio's most unusual features are its railroad tracks and its 22-foot-high double doors. French incorporated these elements to gain access to full sunlight, which affects the appearance of sculpture differently than indoor lighting. This is a particular concern of sculptors who design work for exterior display. When the double doors and the trap doors covering the five-foot-gauge tracks were opened, two or three assistants could push a flatcar bearing the sculpture outside for French to study. The first statue that French executed in his new studio was an equestrian figure of Gen. George Washington holding a raised sword, now at the Place d'Iena in Paris. The statue measured just

The Barn Sculpture Gallery with the "Milmore Memorial" (1889–93) in the background. (Russell C. Hamilton)

Working model for "George Washington" (1896–1900), the first statue that French executed in his new studio. (Russell C. Hamilton)

Casts of his sculpture fill French's studio. (Russell C. Hamilton)

under 22 feet from the horse's hoof to the sword's tip.

In 1900–01, French replaced the Warner farmhouse with a two-story Georgian Revival-style house, also designed by Henry Bacon. Paneling, doors and a mantel from the Warner house were used in the sculptor's office in the new house, and the sitting room is a replica of one in the French family homestead in Chester, N.H.

In 1872, Ralph Waldo Emerson, a family friend, helped French obtain his first major commission, the "Minute Man." This was to be erected at the North Bridge for the centennial of the Concord fight. Although he was then an unknown sculptor, French created one of the most famous American statues ever made. As models, he used himself, a cast of the "Apollo Belvedere" and his father's hired man. In 1874, after studying for a short time with William Rimmer and J.Q.A. Ward, French sailed to Europe for formal training—and missed the unveiling of the "Minute Man."

In 1876, French returned to the United States, working in such places as Washington, D.C., New York City and Cornish, N.H. (where Augustus Saint-Gaudens had a studio). In 1888, French married his cousin Mary Adams French. Ten years later, he created Chesterwood, his home and studio for three decades.

In 1913, when Henry Bacon was given the commission for the Lincoln Memorial, he secured his friend French as sculptor of the memorial. The sculptor's experiments with the statue, originally intended to be 10 feet high, showed that it would be dwarfed and out of scale in the massive hall that Bacon had conceived. French revised his plan accordingly and nearly doubled the statue to its present dimensions. Made of Georgian white marble, the statue was unveiled on May 30, 1922. Plaster casts of two versions of the "Seated Lincoln" are on exhibit in the studio.

After French's death in 1931, his wife continued to use Chesterwood as her summer residence. When she died in 1939, the property became the residence of their daughter, Margaret French Cresson. Under her direction, the barn—the only remaining building from the original working farm French purchased—was remodeled into an exhibition gallery by Helen Douglass French, AIA, and the grounds landscaped by Prentiss French, FASLA. In 1969, Margaret Cresson donated the property to the National Trust in memory of her father. Chesterwood is both a National Historic Landmark and a Massachusetts Historic Landmark.

Today, sketches and working models of French's works are on display in the studio and

the nearby Barn Sculpture Gallery. They include the "Alma Mater" (1903) from the Low Library at Columbia University, the "Brooklyn" and the "Manhattan" groups (1915) for New York City's Manhattan Bridge and the "Dupont Memorial Fountain" (1917) in Washington, D.C. In addition, the collections include works by other well-known American sculptors including Thomas Ball, Evelyn Longman, Augustus Lukeman, Augustus Saint-Gaudens and Margaret French Cresson. The studio also presents French's working environment with materials, notebooks, sketches and tools.

In keeping with its rich artistic heritage, the property presents programs to enhance public appreciation and understanding of American sculpture, including a sculptor-in-residence series. Tours, special events and exhibitions focus on the interpretation of Daniel Chester French's art and an explanation of his working methods in the environment he created. Today, the Berkshire area is home to more than 30 American sculptors, including artists of international as well as regional prominence. A recent exhibition installed contemporary works by area sculptors on the historic grounds of French's estate.

Chesterwood is approximately two miles west of Stockbridge, Mass., on Routes 102 and 183.

For more information, write: Administrator, Chesterwood, Box 248, Stockbridge, Mass. 01262.

French's studio seen from his garden, framing "Andromeda," the culminating work in the sculptor's career. (Paul Rocheleau)

Lyndhurst

Lyndhurst, overlooking the Hudson River's Tappan Zee from a promontory below Tarrytown, N.Y., represents the culmination of Gothic Revival architecture in America. The estate was shaped over 140 years by three families, the Pauldings, the Merritts and the Goulds. Their influence is still to be seen—in the house, expanded from a country villa "in the pointed style" to a Gothic mansion; in its rich furnishings and mementoes; and in its grounds, landscaped in the picturesque mode of the 19th century.

Alexander Jackson Davis (1803–92), one of America's most influential architects, designed Lyndhurst in 1838 for William Paulding. Originally called Paulding Manor, the house was a retirement home for Paulding, who had served as a general in the War of 1812 and was a mayor of New York.

The 1830s were a time of political and technological change leading to an industrial aristocracy in America. Romanticism dominated the arts, and the Hudson River Valley became a center of romantic painting and architecture. Wealthy patrons commissioned elaborate mansions like Paulding Manor in a variety of picturesque styles along the bluff of the river, from New York City to Albany.

Portrait of former owner Jay Gould over the fireplace in the first-floor office at Lyndhurst. (Jack E. Boucher, Historic American Buildings Survey)

*Antique and classic cars parade during a show at
Lyndhurst. (Karas Photo)*

Picturesque architecture was a reaction to the symmetry and order of earlier classical styles. In contrast to Greek Revival designs, for example, the typical romantic house had an informal plan with asymmetrical massing of towers, wings and bays.

Architect Davis observed of this style: "The English collegiate [Gothic] style is for many reasons to be preferred. It admits of greater variety of plans and outline ... while its bay windows, oriels, turrets, and chimney shafts give a pictorial effect."

Paulding Manor, constructed of gray-white Sing-Sing marble, was the first of a series of houses that came to be called Hudson River Gothic. Joined to the landscape by broad porches and verandas, the building is rich in Gothic details, including arched doors and windows, ribbed and vaulted ceilings, figured bosses and Gothic furniture designed by Davis.

Davis doubled the size of the mansion in 1864–65 for its second owner, New York merchant George Merritt, who renamed the estate Lyndhurst. The roofline was raised, and a new wing, a porte-cochere and an imposing tower were added.

Merritt died in 1873. Seven years later, the estate was purchased as a summer home by railroad magnate Jay Gould, who epitomized the Gilded Age of unrestrained capitalism.

Gould's daughter Helen, who later married Finley J. Shepard, was given charge of the property on her father's death in 1892. She was involved in numerous philanthropic works, and during her lifetime the gates of Lyndhurst frequently were opened to young people who came to study or enjoy parties. On her death in 1938, her sister, Anna, Duchess of Talleyrand-Perigord, returned from France to live at Lyndhurst. She died in 1961, and through her generosity the 67-acre estate passed to the National Trust.

The furnishings and decorations of the mansion reflect the lifestyles of the three families: the Pauldings' early Gothic, the Merritts' High Victorian Gothic and the French 18th-century and Beaux-Arts styles favored by the Goulds.

The Gothic-style chairs and tables in the main hallway were designed by Davis for General Paulding, while the marbelized painting of the walls and ceilings and the blue and white marble floor are changes Davis made for George Merritt. The Paulding dining room became the library when Merritt added the north wing.

The principal room of Merritt's addition was the dining room. Gothic woodwork, red stenciled walls and Gothic dining room furniture, all designed by Davis, appear now as they were in 1867.

Originally lined with Gothic bookcases, the art gallery on the second floor was the outstanding room of the Paulding house. Both Merritt and Gould used the room as a combination art gallery and billiard room. Paintings today have been rehung according to documents of the 1890s.

The grounds at Lyndhurst are important examples of 19th-century American landscape architecture and complement the picturesque mansion.

Merritt directed the construction of a mammoth greenhouse, topped with a great Saracen cupola, but after he died it fell into disrepair. Jay Gould refitted and restocked the greenhouse, but it was destroyed by fire just months after his acquisition of the property. Gould rebuilt the structure, commissioning greenhouse designers Lord and Burnham to double its size, and restocked it with plants from around the world. Today, partial stabilization suggests the grandeur of one of the largest private greenhouses ever built.

Among other modifications to the property, Jay Gould constructed a pier on the river as a mooring for *The Atalanta,* the yacht he used to commute to New York City.

Helen Gould Shepard continued Lyndhurst's building program, adding kennels, a Shingle-style recreation building that contains a

Jay Gould's Wooten patent desk was an addition to the mansion's furnishings during the Gould ownership. (Jack E. Boucher, Historic American Buildings Survey)

The dining room, furnished with the Gothic furniture designed for the room by A.J. Davis. The walls are painted plaster with a stenciled floral pattern covered with a red glaze. (Louis H. Frohman)

regulation-size bowling alley, a pavilion enclosing one of the largest indoor swimming tanks of that period and the Rose Cottage, a playhouse for the Shepards' adopted children. She also dedicated considerable energy to improving the landscape, manifested in the formal rose garden, and to stimulating local interest in horticulture.

In 1966, Lyndhurst was designated a National Historic Landmark. The National Trust now operates it as a historic house museum, promoting the history, culture and preservation of the Hudson River Valley. Period room exhibits illustrate life at Lyndhurst in the 19th century. The historic site is the setting for concerts, lectures, special events and horticultural programs. Through preservation of the waterfront at Lyndhurst and the property's expanse of open space, the National Trust encourages similar conservation efforts along the Hudson.

From its Restoration Workshop located at Lyndhurst, the National Trust provides on-site restoration work for its own properties as well as those of other preservation organizations.

Lyndhurst is located on South Broadway (U.S. Route 9) in Tarrytown, N.Y.

For more information, write: Administrator, Lyndhurst, 635 South Broadway, Tarrytown, N.Y. 10591.

Aerial view of the Gothic castlelike property along the Hudson River. (Jack E. Boucher, Historic American Buildings Survey)

1881 view of the Lyndhurst greenhouse, at the time the largest in the world. (Historic American Buildings Survey)

Cliveden

For more than 200 years, Cliveden has withstood onslaughts from the Battle of Germantown during the American Revolution to the urban encroachments of today. Benjamin Chew, distinguished Philadelphia lawyer, jurist and political leader, had the stately Georgian country home called Cliveden built near Philadelphia between 1763 and 1767. Today a historic house museum, this National Historic Landmark is a six-acre oasis in the bustling community of Germantown, six miles northeast of center-city Philadelphia. With its elegant 18th and 19th-century furnishings, Cliveden is a contemporary reminder of a way of life during the era of Benjamin Chew.

Chew was born in colonial Maryland to Quaker parents. His father, Samuel Chew, a successful physician and lawyer, was later appointed chief justice of the "lower counties" (now Delaware) by the Penn Proprietors. Benjamin Chew was sent to Philadelphia to study law in the office of Andrew Hamilton. He continued his studies at London's Middle Temple, and on his return to this country was admitted to the bar of the Supreme Court of Pennsylvania.

Chew became a powerful ally of the Penn Proprietors. In 1755, he was appointed attorney general, and a succession of public offices followed: recorder of Philadelphia, speaker of the Assembly of the Lower Counties, registrar general, member of council and in 1774, chief justice of Pennsylvania. Combined with his private practice in law, this meant not only prominence as a public figure, but also wealth.

In the English tradition, Chew decided to build a country home appropriate to his social position.

Chew had spent the summer of 1763 in Germantown at Mount Airy, the estate of his friend Judge William Allen. Finding the area agreeable, Chew acquired 11 acres nearby on Germantown Road. He secured the services of mason John Hesser, master carpenter Jacob Knor and stonecutter Caspar Guyer. From architectural drawings and building accounts among the Chew papers, it is apparent that Chew himself played a significant part in the design and building of the house. Construction required four years.

The mansion displays many of the Palladian elements incorporated in fashionable English houses of the period but modified by colonial American tastes and means. Cliveden is a two-and-one-half-story structure built of locally cut stone with five evenly placed bays across the facade. The slightly projecting center pavilion with a pedimented door frame and fluted

Main entrance of Cliveden. (Cortlandt Hubbard, Historic American Buildings Survey)

Entrance hall, separated by a screen of columns from the stair hall at rear. (Jack E. Boucher, Historic American Buildings Survey)

The parlor, whose features include a chimney breast with a tabernacle frame and a marble-faced fireplace. (Jack E. Boucher, Historic American Buildings Survey)

Cliveden in a painting of the 1777 Battle of Germantown by E.L. Henry, which hangs in the entrance hall. (National Trust)

columns supports a full classical entablature. The urns on the roof, imported from England, were a source of great pride to Chew and were "suitable to the plainness of [his] building." Symmetry dictated flanking service dependencies at the rear and a balanced interior plan. Classical details were employed also in the interior ornamentation, including broken pedimented door frames and a screen of four columns with a fully developed entablature that divides the entrance from the stair hall.

As the Revolution approached, the chief justice's position as an official of the Crown became tenuous. Rather than take a political position while on the bench, Chew seems to have remained faithful to the principles of law. On April 10, 1776, he gave his notable charge to the Grand Jury of Pennsylvania: "I have stated that an opposition of force of arms to the lawful authority of the King or his ministers ... is High Treason; but in the moment when the King or his ministers shall exceed their constitutional authority ... submission to their mandates becomes Treason."

As the British were moving toward Philadelphia in the summer of 1777, the First City Troop arrested Chew and confined him with Gov. John Penn at Union Forge in northern New Jersey. He remained there until the British occupation of Philadelphia ended the following spring.

Meanwhile, on the morning of October 4, 1777, English forces and Gen. George Washington's men engaged in the major confrontation of the Battle of Germantown at Cliveden. The building's stone construction prevented the American troops from breaching the walls of the British-held residence with their cannon, and Washington was forced to retreat.

But the effects on Cliveden were serious. Its contents were largely destroyed, and the fabric of the house was severely damaged. When Chew returned the next year, he found it "an absolute wreck, and materials not to be had to keep out the weather." No doubt uncertain of his own future, he found it inadvisable to restore Cliveden to its former state. In 1779, he sold the country home to Blair McClenachen, a young merchant from Ireland.

Hostilities abated, and it was evident that Chew had not conspired with nor supported the British cause. He was called to fill another important judicial position, president of the High Court of Errors and Appeals for the commonwealth of Pennsylvania. He held that position from 1791 until his retirement 17 years later at the age of 85. In 1797, he repurchased Cliveden, and it remained in the Chew family continuously to the present generation. In June 1972, the Chew family donated the property to the National Trust. A barn adjacent to the house was restored in 1976 to be used for public meetings and lectures to make Cliveden a community preservation center in its neighborhood.

Cliveden today is richly furnished with Philadelphia mahogany furniture, some of which was once owned by Gov. John Penn and is attributed to the workshop of Thomas Affleck. Other pieces were made by cabinetmakers Jonathan Gostelowe and David Evans. Family portraits were painted by John Smibert, John Wollaston and Robert Edge Pine. Original fabrics, clothing and Benjamin Chew's law library also have survived in their original setting.

Cliveden is richly documented, with an estimated 200,000 manuscript pages making up the Chew papers, which document two centuries of Chew family life. The ongoing study of these valuable sources continues to reveal more and more of Cliveden's past and its historical relationship to Philadelphia and to the nation.

Cliveden is located at 6401 Germantown Avenue. From Wissahickon Drive (through Fairmount Park), take Johnson Street, going east to the intersection of Germantown Avenue.

For more information, write: Administrator, Cliveden, 6401 Germantown Avenue, Philadelphia, Pa. 19144.

Decatur House

In 1818, when Decatur House was being built, Washington was only a small city of 9,000, essentially rural with dirt roads and carriage ruts criss-crossing open spaces. This visual simplicity was deceptive, however, for life was already as complicated as one might expect in a national capital. As surely as Maj. Pierre L'Enfant had prepared a physical plan, Washington's social and political patterns were being laid down as well.

Decatur House was erected as the first private residence on Lafayette Square (then called President's Square) within view of both St. John's Church and the White House. Commissioned by Commodore Stephen Decatur and designed by Benjamin Henry Latrobe, it was planned as a place where the owner could become the center of social and political life of the federal city.

Decatur's fame as a naval hero added to this likelihood. Born to a Philadelphia seafaring family, Decatur had risen quickly through the ranks of the United States Navy. In the Barbary Wars of 1804, he had led a score of volunteers on a midnight raid in Tripoli Harbor, burning the pirate-held U.S. frigate *Philadelphia.* British naval hero Lord Nelson hailed this exploit as "the most bold and daring act of the age." As reward, Decatur was promoted to the rank of captain at the age of 26. Later, during the War of 1812, Decatur was again commended for his capture of H.M.S. *Macedonia.*

Commissioning Latrobe to design his private residence only added to Decatur's prestige. Latrobe's position as the most notable architect of the era was well established. He had recently been commissioned to redesign the U.S. Capitol after its burning in 1814, and he designed St. John's Church in 1816.

For Decatur House, Latrobe chose the English town house style as the basic concept, overlaid with Adamesque (or Federal) influence. As was the custom, the family living quarters and the master bedroom were on the first floor, drawing rooms on the second and guest rooms on the third. The kitchen, stables and servants' quarters were all outbuildings.

Latrobe's use of classical elements to create an austere beauty is most evident in the vestibule, which served as the formal entrance. The vaulted ceiling, divided into three segments, contains a rectangle, a circle and a hemisphere, front to back. The semicircular shape is repeated in molding and curved wooden doors opening onto a winding stairway. Symmetrical balance is preserved through the use of false doors in both the vestibule and the second-floor landing, sophisticated design devices of Latrobe.

A late 18th century photo.

*In the entrance hall of Decatur House, three
geometric forms—the rectangle, circle and
semicircle—create a harmonious design.
(Marler Photo)*

Early in 1819 Decatur moved in and immediately set about entertaining Washington society. This new phase of Decatur's career was short-lived, however. He was mortally wounded in March 1820 in a duel with Commodore James Barron. Barron believed that Decatur had been instrumental in barring him from returning to active naval duty following disciplinary action.

For the next 40 years, Decatur House was a home and a meeting place for some of the most important politicians and diplomats in American history. Foreign ministers from three leading world powers—France, Russia and England—set up residence in the house. Henry Clay, Martin Van Buren and Edward Livingston all lived in the house while serving as secretary of state, then considered to be a stepping stone to the presidency.

In 1842, the house was purchased by hotelier John Gadsby. After Gadsby's death in 1844, Vice President George Dallas rented the house from the hotelier's estate. The last resident before the Civil War was Judah P. Benjamin, who lived there while serving as senator from Louisiana.

The Civil War brought a new era to Washington. People flooded the city from all directions, and thousands of soldiers were stationed in and around the District. The government took possession of Decatur House in 1862, using it for storage and possibly living quarters. The elegant structure fell into disrepair after seven years of government occupation.

In 1871, the house was purchased by Mary Edwards Beale, wife of Gen. Edward Fitzgerald Beale. The general, seeking a home in the District to complement his California ranch, was as romantic and accomplished as Decatur had been. With Kit Carson in 1848, he had carried from California to Washington the news of American victories in the Mexican War and the accession of California. Within months, as a courier for the U.S. Navy, Beale again undertook the dangerous crossing of the continent, secretly passing through Mexico, this time to bring Washington the first samples of California gold. And in the 1850s, he became commander of the U.S. Camel Corps, designed to use camels imported from Tunis as pack animals across the American Southwest desert. Demonstrating such creativity, Beale became a favorite of the Lincoln and Grant administrations, the latter sending him to Austria as ambassador.

Before the Beales moved into Decatur House, a major refurbishing took place. They introduced Victorian features by adding sandstone trim around the entrance and the first-floor windows and installing gaslights. Ceilings were frescoed with floral designs and parquetry flooring was laid in the drawing room,

where the California state seal is depicted in rare California woods. The servants' quarters were extended, and a one-story conservatory was added to the south side of the house. Once work was completed, Decatur House again became a social center for the wealthiest and most powerful in Washington society.

Upon Beale's death in 1893, his son, Truxtun, became master of the house. Truxtun Beale led a diverse life. As a diplomat, he opened trade relations with Turkey and Persia. As a writer, he expounded on the theories of Herbert Spencer. As a philanthropist, he gave much to charity. And as a personality, his humor and wit were shown in unpredictable ways.

After Truxtun's death in 1936, his wife, Marie, became concerned about the future of Decatur House. In 1937, 1945 and 1950, public efforts were needed to stop demolition of the house. Marie Beale was always on the front line, battling government officials and contractors who saw the site as a place to put their next office building. In 1944, Mrs. Beale retained architect Thomas T. Waterman to restore the house according to the original Latrobe designs. Twelve years later, she bequeathed Decatur House to the National Trust.

Designated a National Historic Landmark in 1961, the house is now a vital element in the restoration of Lafayette Square. Historic buildings

Entrance to Decatur House facing Lafayette Square. (Marler Photo)

Stephen Decatur's bedroom on the first floor, with a portrait of the naval hero. (National Trust)

facing the square were saved from demolition intended to make way for two new federal office buildings. Instead, early buildings were restored and several new residential-style structures were constructed, while the major office complexes were accommodated within the blocks behind the streetfronts, in red brick mirroring that of Decatur House.

Today, the National Trust operates Decatur House as a historic house museum focusing on its illustrious occupants. The furnishings of the first floor have been restored to the styles popular during Decatur's lifetime and include some of his original furniture and mementoes of his naval career. The second floor now reflects the Victorian tastes of the Beale family. Together, these period rooms represent more than 150 years of life on Lafayette Square.

Until 1979, Decatur House also served as headquarters for the National Trust, its third floor adapted for office use. The Preservation Bookshop of the National Trust is now housed in the former servants' wing, where it offers several thousand books and gifts for preservationists.

Decatur House is located at 748 Jackson Place, N.W., in downtown Washington, D.C., one block north of the White House.

For more information, write: Administrator, Decatur House, 748 Jackson Place, N.W., Washington, D.C. 20006.

South drawing room on the second floor, with its Beale furnishings including an 18th-century Portuguese table, ceiling frescoed in a floral design and a large gaselier. (Jack E. Boucher, Historic American Buildings Survey)

The second-floor stair hall, looking out over an enclosed urban garden. Details designed by Latrobe include a curved stairwell, oval recessed ceiling and a false door at the left. (Marler Photo)

Entrance to the Woodrow Wilson House shows its
Palladian-style windows and porch to the right.
(Marler Photo)

Woodrow Wilson House

When Woodrow Wilson left the White House in 1921, he moved to a red brick Georgian Revival town house on a quiet street in Washington's embassy district. He remained there until his death in 1924. His wife, Edith Bolling Galt Wilson, continued to live in the house until 1961. During these 37 years, she carefully preserved the building, its furnishings and the varied mementoes of her husband's personal life and long public career. Upon her death in 1961, she bequeathed the property to the American people under the guardianship of the National Trust. Today, operated as a historic house museum, Wilson House is the only former president's home in the nation's capital open to the public—a time capsule of life and lifestyles in the 1920s.

Thomas Woodrow Wilson was born in 1856 in Staunton, Va. His father, Joseph Ruggles Wilson, a Scottish immigrant, was a printer turned Presbyterian minister; his mother, English-born Jessie Woodrow, was the daughter of a Presbyterian minister. Two years after his birth, Wilson's family moved to Augusta, Ga. It was there that the adolescent Wilson saw the ravages of war first hand; his father's church was used as a hospital during the Civil War, the church yard as a stockade.

At the age of 17, Wilson entered Davidson College, but withdrew because of ill health. He returned to college two years later, enrolling in Princeton. Venturing north of the Mason-Dixon line for the first time, Wilson studied political science and was active in debate and oratory clubs.

After graduation, he read law at the University of Virginia and subsequently opened a law office in the booming city of Atlanta. Wilson, however, enjoyed the philosophy of law, not the practice. He spent most of his time listening to debates in the Georgia legislature and had few clients. Terminating his moribund practice, Wilson decided on a career as a college professor. Receiving his doctorate from the Johns Hopkins University in Baltimore, Wilson went to teach at Bryn Mawr College in Pennsylvania. Anxious to teach men, Wilson moved in 1888 to Wesleyan University in Connecticut and two years later back to Princeton. There he stayed for 20 years, lecturing on political science and history and serving for eight years as the university's president. As president of Princeton, Wilson labored to create a school exalting the intellectual, rather than one simply teaching people how to earn a living. New Jersey citizens rapidly came to view him as a progressive educator, struggling at the Ivy League school against privilege and vested interest.

In 1910, Wilson accepted the offer of the New Jersey Democratic leaders to run for governor and was elected. Battling the political machine that got him elected, Wilson quickly gained national prominence as "the most hopeful figure in American politics." Two years after being elected to his first public office, Wilson was elected president of the United States, defeating Republican incumbent William Howard Taft and former President Theodore Roosevelt.

During his administration, Wilson guided many progressive reforms through Congress and signed numerous others passed by progressive legislators. Of particular note are the Underwood Tariff (1913), which lowered or eliminated duties on several products; the Federal Reserve System (1913), which created a new centralized banking system; and the Federal Trade Commission (1914), which provided for the supervision of interstate trade practices. During these years, Wilson also entwined the United States in the volatile domestic politics of Santo Domingo, Haiti, Nicaragua and Mexico, while he also faced a war looming on the European horizon.

Twenty months after Wilson's first wife died, he married Edith Bolling Galt, the widow of a prominent Washington jeweler.

In 1917, one month after his second inauguration, Wilson called for a declaration of war against Germany and quickly mobilized the country's resources. Eight months later, he outlined his plan for peace, "The Fourteen Points," promoting free trade, providing self-determination and establishing a League of Nations. The plan, he hoped, would provide for international stability and peace, allowing the United States to expand its economy through international trade.

Soon after the Armistice was signed on November 11, 1918, the president sailed to Europe, to the Paris Peace Conference, in hopes of selling his program for peace. At the conference, Wilson compromised on many important issues to gain the support of England, France and Italy on the League of Nations issue. The creation of the League, he believed, would mitigate any problems arising from his compromises.

Through his efforts, a covenant establishing a League was finally included in the Treaty of Versailles. Once at home, however, Wilson saw the Senate refuse to ratify the treaty, thereby denying the United States membership in the League. Wilson decided to carry his arguments to the people and arranged a nationwide speaking tour. Already tired from the Paris Conference, however, Wilson was exhausted by his tour. On September 25, as he turned eastward from the Pacific Coast, the president

The library reflects Wilson's scholarly nature and the many gifts made to him from around the world. Wilson spent much of his time in the house here. (Marler Photo)

The president's bedroom at Wilson House. (National Trust)

collapsed. He spent the remainder of his term as president inactive and recuperating with the help of Edith Wilson.

On Inauguration Day 1921, President and Mrs. Wilson left the White House for the last time. After attending the Capitol ceremonies for President Harding, they drove directly to their new home on S Street. Wilson had wanted to build a house from his own plans (a sketch hangs on the wall of his bedroom), but could not afford it. The couple also considered the advantages of retiring to several East Coast cities—New York, Boston, Richmond, Baltimore or Washington. "Eventually," Mrs. Wilson recalled, "Washington was decided on [because] the Library of Congress afforded the facilities which my husband wishes to use while writing a book he had long had in mind and [because] it was home to me."

Mrs. Wilson spent several weeks looking at available houses in the city. The red brick town house designed in 1915 by architect Waddy B. Wood for Henry Fairbanks was the only one that appealed to her. According to her later description, it was "an unpretentious, comfortable, dignified house, fitted to the needs of a gentleman." She told her husband about her find, but was completely surprised when, on their fifth wedding anniversary, he took her to the house and, following a Scottish custom,

presented her with a piece of sod from the garden and the key to the front door.

Wilson spent his retirement years reflecting on his long scholarly and political career. He also received numerous visitors—statesmen from abroad such as David Lloyd George, politicians such as Cordell Hull and Carter Glass—and enjoyed his library of more than 8,000 books.

It was a quiet life. Meals were taken in the library or in the solarium. With Mrs. Wilson, the president enjoyed frequent motor rides through Rock Creek Park, along the Potomac and into Virginia. He regularly enjoyed movies, plays and vaudeville at Keith's, Poli's and the National Theatre.

Now a house museum, Wilson House is open for tours on a regular basis. It also offers temporary exhibits, school tours and such special events as the annual Armistice Day celebration and a 1920s Christmas. These programs provide insight into the life and times of Woodrow Wilson, one of this country's most influential and leading statesmen.

Wilson House is located at 2340 S Street in northwest Washington, D.C., off Massachusetts Avenue, two blocks north of Sheridan Circle.

For more information, write: Administrator, Wilson House, 2340 S Street, N.W., Washington, D.C. 20008.

Woodlawn Plantation

Woodlawn has been a home, a working plantation and the hub of an active community in northern Virginia for nearly two centuries. Its occupants have included the granddaughter of Martha Washington, Quaker and Baptist settlers from the North, a playwright and a U.S. senator. Throughout, Woodlawn has been a vital community of people and places, constantly changing and developing.

The plantation, carved from George Washington's Mount Vernon estate, was a gift to his foster daughter, Eleanor Parke Custis, and his nephew, Lawrence Lewis. Eleanor, who was known as Nelly, and Lawrence were married at Mount Vernon on February 22, 1799, Washington's last birthday. The General set aside 2,000 acres of Mount Vernon lands—including Dogue Run Farm, a gristmill and a distillery—for the Lewises.

Dr. William Thornton, the first architect of the U.S. Capitol, was engaged to design the mansion. Construction was begun around 1800. The wings were completed in 1803, and in that year the Lewises moved to Woodlawn. When the center block was completed in 1805, the house incorporated architectural elements reminiscent of Kenmore, Lewis's childhood home, and was furnished primarily with pieces from Mount

Vernon. A swath of trees was cut away in front of the river entrance to the mansion to afford a view of Mount Vernon and the Potomac River. The river bound the two estates together and provided a link between them and to other northern Virginia houses that grew up along its shores in the early 19th century.

After the death of Lawrence Lewis in 1839, Nelly moved to her son Lorenzo's home in Clarke County, Va., and Woodlawn was left vacant. In 1846, after seven years of neglect, it was put up for public sale. The estate at this time included the mansion and 2,030 acres.

Woodlawn's timber and arable land attracted Jacob and Paul Hillman Troth and Chalkley and Lucas Gillingham, suppliers of ship timber and tanning bark to the Philadelphia market. The Troths and Gillinghams, who were Quakers, also recognized in Woodlawn's acres an opportunity to provide farmland to settlers from the North who would farm with free, rather than slave, labor. The setting was further enhanced by the proximity of the Potomac River, an important transportation route.

The four men formed the Troth-Gillingham Company. After purchasing the rundown estate, they oversaw the sale of Woodlawn lands and those of surrounding plantations for small farms. In addition to developing their farms, the settlers designed boats to carry passengers on the

The river facade of Woodlawn. (Del Ankers)

The ornithological interests of Lorenzo Lewis, the only surviving Lewis son, can be seen in his bedroom. (Frederick E. Paton)

Potomac and to run the creeks and river transporting Woodlawn's products to the ports of Alexandria and Philadelphia.

Shortly after the Troth-Gillingham Company purchase, John and Rachel Mason purchased the house and 500 acres from the company. The Masons, who were Baptists, were deeply religious—like their Quaker neighbors—and organized a Sunday school in their home and later a church nearby.

Both John and Rachel Mason died by 1889 and were buried at Woodlawn Baptist Church. The Woodlawn estate was divided equally among their children, but only Otis Tufton Mason established even a part-time residence there. Mason, a noted scholar and lecturer, lived in Washington, D.C., but frequently spent weekends and summers at Woodlawn.

Because the Mason children were all well established when their parents died and none wished to make a permanent move to Woodlawn, the mansion was sold in 1892 to the New Alexandria Land and River Improvement Company, a firm that was developing a new town near Alexandria. The company also had begun work on a trolley to carry tourists to Mount Vernon, and they proposed that the line be extended to Woodlawn.

The firm's plans were never realized, however. In a period of two days in September 1896, a devastating hurricane struck the area. Woodlawn, standing alone and unprotected, sustained considerable damage. Trees near the house were blown down, shutters and windows were broken and part of the roof was torn off. Although some repairs to the house were made, the effects of the storm and the bleak financial outlook for the trolley caused the company to abandon its efforts.

Once again, Woodlawn was put up for sale. Paul Kester, a young New York City playwright, bought the badly deteriorated structure in 1901, began repair work immediately and soon moved in with his brother, mother and 60 cats. This purchase probably saved the mansion from eventual demolition by neglect.

During their four-year residence, the Kester brothers oversaw continuing repairs to the house while they pursued their literary careers. In addition to their repair work, the Kesters also made several structural and ornamental changes. Most notably, they raised the wings and hyphens to accommodate the addition of modern conveniences.

The Kesters sold Woodlawn in 1905. The new owner, Elizabeth Sharpe of Pennsylvania, set out to accurately restore the house to its original appearance and, in the course of her 20-year residence, spent $100,000 on the project. She hired two Washington architects, Waddy B. Wood

The music room at Woodlawn is the largest and most elegant room in the house, showing the importance of music to the Lewises. (Frederick E. Paton)

Gazebo in the Woodlawn gardens, restored by the Garden Club of Virginia. (Marler Photo)

and later Edward W. Donn, Jr., to oversee the work.

Sharpe's restoration work included alteration of some of the Kester changes that she considered inappropriate. She tore down the wings and hyphens because the bricks, windows and entrances were not in harmony with the rest of the house. But in rebuilding these features, she disregarded the architects' advice to restore them to their original form, choosing instead to retain the increased space created by the Kesters.

With the acquisition of additional land, Elizabeth Sharpe brought the estate to roughly its present size of 136 acres. She planted a formal garden patterned on 18th-century prototypes and also installed the boxwood in front of the river entrance.

Sharpe died in 1925, and Woodlawn was purchased by Sen. and Mrs. Oscar Underwood of Alabama. The senator and his wife, Bertha, continued the restoration begun by Woodlawn's previous owners, hiring Waddy Wood to work on the dining room and to create a landscape plan for the grounds.

After the senator died in January 1929, his widow continued to live in the house periodically until 1935, when she rented it to Secretary of War and Mrs. Harry W. Woodring. During the Woodring residence, the house was the site of many social events and conferences. Mrs.

Underwood returned to Woodlawn in 1937, and the house remained in the Underwood family until her death in 1948.

Public ownership of Woodlawn began in that year when the estate was purchased by the Woodlawn Public Foundation. It was operated by the National Trust for nine years under a lease agreement with the foundation until 1957, when ownership passed to the National Trust.

Woodlawn, now more than 175 years old and operated as a historic house museum, reflects the many periods of its history. Lewis-era period rooms are on display in the original 1805 portion of the house. The wings and hyphens date from the first quarter of the 20th century and are used for educational programs, special events and a preservation shop. In addition to public tours and school programs, the National Trust sponsors several annual events such as a nationally known needlework exhibit and period Christmas celebrations. It is through these varied programs that Woodlawn works to promote and foster appreciation of the history and culture of northern Virginia.

Woodlawn is located on U.S. Route 1, 14 miles south of Washington, D.C. It is also 3 miles west of Mount Vernon via the George Washington Memorial Parkway.

For more information, write: Administrator, Woodlawn, Mount Vernon, Va. 22121.

The main hall, with portraits of George and Martha Washington. (Frederick E. Paton)

The bedroom originally used by the Lewis girls. (Frederick E. Paton)

The Pope-Leighey House

"The house of moderate cost is not only America's major architectural problem but the problem most difficult for her major architects," said Frank Lloyd Wright in 1938. "As for me, I would rather solve it with satisfaction to myself and Usonia, than build anything I can think of...." Such thinking inspired Wright to create the Usonian house, a series of houses designed in the 1940s "to give the little family the benefit of industrial advantages of the era." ("Usonia" was English author Samuel Butler's proposed name for the United States.)

In August 1939, after reading Wright's *An Autobiography,* Loren Pope asked the architect to design a Usonian home for his plot of virgin timberland in Falls Church, Va.

With anticipation, Pope awaited the reply: "Dear Loren, of course I'm ready to give you a house...."

Wright visited the site several times during construction. Gordon Chadwick, an apprentice from Wright's Taliesin Fellowship, served as construction supervisor. Less than a year and a half from the initial request, the Popes moved into their new home. It cost them approximately $8,000.

The Pope-Leighey House, built in 1940, is one of Wright's early Usonian houses and illustrates the hallmarks of his architectural philosophy. As with his early Prairie houses, the living quarters are treated as a spatial unity, not compartmentalized into a series of boxes. Except where privacy is required in the bedrooms and the bath, walls and doors are eliminated. The remaining space, far from being left open as a vast area, is subtly and ingeniously defined in ways to establish specific uses for various areas and to control how they are used. A fireplace is included, not for heat but for the psychological values of warmth, protection and family unity. Furniture—to the degree possible—is Wright-designed and built in.

The exterior of the house conforms clearly to the interior space. The basement and attic are eliminated, the functions of heating and storage incorporated elsewhere in the house. The roof is flat and close to the ground, enhancing the sense of shelter by a broad and substantial overhang. The building's height is reduced to the scale of human figures. All doors and window openings are brought into line and harmonized by emphasizing their horizontal continuity. And the house is set sensitively into its natural environment, not put on it.

The Pope-Leighey House also demonstrates Wright's concern for providing moderately priced housing. A number of its features, unusual for the time, have become accepted in many houses

Overview of the house, sited sensitively in its new
location. (Jack E. Boucher, Historic American
Buildings Survey)

Entrance driveway with overhanging carport. The
distinctive cutout design in the clerestory can be
seen at left. (Wm. Edmund Barrett)

today. It is built on a concrete slab with heating pipes imbedded. Only three primary materials were used: cypress, brick and glass. Walls are constructed of cypress sheathing screwed to both sides of a plywood core. There is no ornamentation that is not indigenous to the materials themselves—in the way they are cut, joined, fitted together; the forms and shapes they make; and their individual colors and textures as seen alone or juxtaposed.

In 1946, Mr. and Mrs. Robert Leighey of Richmond discovered that the Popes' house was for sale. Familiar with Wright's work and architectural philosophy, the Leigheys visited the site. They immediately loved it, soon after bought it and for 17 years enjoyed it.

"I think you become a better person by living here," said Mrs. Leighey. "Little by little your pretensions fall away and you become a more truthful, a more honest person." The Leigheys felt privileged to own the house and shared it with all the curious who arrived unannounced.

In December 1963, however, Mrs. Leighey received notice from the commonwealth of Virginia that it intended to use her property in the construction of Interstate 66. Mrs. Leighey, whose husband had died six months before, vowed to save her home. She contacted the National Trust for Historic Preservation and the U.S. Department of the Interior, hoping that either might come to the rescue. Despite valiant efforts by the National Trust, the Secretary of the Interior and numerous other preservation groups, the Virginia Department of Highways could not be convinced to reroute the road. The only alternative to demolition was relocation.

Mrs. Leighey donated the property to the National Trust along with the $31,500 condemnation payment. These funds, supplemented by assistance from the American Institute of Architects, three anonymous donors, radio and television stations and local newspapers, allowed the building to be dismantled, moved and reassembled.

The National Park Service supervised the rescue operation in 1964–65, with Taliesin Associated Architects serving as consultants. William Wesley Peters, chief architect of the consulting firm and vice president of the Frank Lloyd Wright Foundation, assisted in the selection of a new site. Of several proposed sites that would have provided a similar natural setting, the National Trust-owned Woodlawn Plantation was selected; it had similar indigenous vegetation and was only 15 miles from the Falls Church location. Howard C. Rickert of Vienna, Va., the master craftsman who originally built the house and furniture, was employed to disassemble and rebuild it. The process took nine months. In June 1965, the

Side of the Pope-Leighey House leading to the living room at the far end. (Jack E. Boucher, Historic American Buildings Survey)

The living room, looking from the hearth to the dining area. (Jack E. Boucher, Historic American Buildings Survey)

Detail on side of house repeating the clerestory pattern. (Jack E. Boucher, Historic American Buildings Survey)

Pope-Leighey House was dedicated at its new site.

Ironically, other challenges to the highway were temporarily successful, and actual construction of Interstate 66 did not begin until 1979.

On its new site at Woodlawn Plantation, the modest suburban house of the mid-20th century offers an instructive contrast with the Georgian-style plantation house of the early 19th century.

"The plan of the Loren Pope house is remarkable for the luxury of space despite its small size," observed Peters. "The entrance to the house with its pair of glass doors, the spacious living room and the eleven foot high ceilings, the liberal use of plate glass, the brick fireplace, the private study and the extended roofs give this building a distinctive character with the new sense of space, light and freedom to which our United States of America is entitled. It is to the citizen of today's democratic society every bit as appropriate as the elegant plantation mansion was to the aristocrat of the pre-war South."

The Pope-Leighey House is located at Woodlawn Plantation, on U.S. Route 1, 14 miles south of Washington, D.C. It is also 3 miles west of Mount Vernon via the George Washington Memorial Parkway.

For more information, write: Administrator, Woodlawn, Mount Vernon, Va. 22121.

Belle Grove is one of the most architecturally distinguished houses in Virginia's Shenandoah Valley. The history and fortunes of the property and the valley have been closely linked since the area's settlement in the first half of the 18th century. Both prospered from the rich land, and both suffered from the devastation and decline brought by the Civil War.

The house was built in the last decade of the 18th century by Maj. Issac Hite. He was a grandson of Jost Hite, who had come from Alsace to Kingston, N.Y., in 1710 with the great emigration of Germans and Swiss who fled their homelands because of wars and heavy taxation.

From Kingston, the Hite family moved to Germantown, Pa., and then to the Shenandoah Valley. Jost Hite and his partner, Robert McKay, had received a grant of 100,000 acres from the Virginia government with the stipulation that 100 families would be settled on the land within two years. In 1732, the Hites, McKay and 16 other families moved to the valley. Lord Fairfax, however, challenged their right to the land, contending that the government did not have the authority to infringe on his vast Northern Neck holdings. The case was settled finally in 1786, and title was granted to Jost Hite's heirs.

Issac Hite received from his father 483 acres of land in Frederick County late in 1782. It was here that he eventually constructed Belle Grove. On January 2, 1783, Hite married Eleanor Conway Madison of Montpelier, Orange County, Va., sister of James Madison.

Through Madison, Thomas Jefferson became involved in the design of Belle Grove. Madison wrote Jefferson in October 1794, explaining: "This will be handed to you by Mr. Bond who is to build a large house for Mr. Hite my brother in law on my suggestion he is to visit Monticello not only to profit of examples before his eyes, but to ask the favor of your advice on the plan of the house. Mr. Hite particularly wishes it [your advice] in what relates to the [bow] room and the portico.... In general, any hints which may occur to you for improving the plan will be thankfully accepted."

Jefferson, whose abilities as an architect have been overshadowed by his political and literary achievements, left his mark on Belle Grove. The plan and concept are far more Jeffersonian than they are characteristic of domestic architecture of the valley. Although containing none of the octagons and ovals for which his spatial concepts are famous, Belle Grove resembles one of Jefferson's favorite versions of a one-story house. The fanlight over the main door easily could have come from his own designs. It is a semicircle with intersecting muntins forming a

*Hay jumping proves popular with children
during Farm Craft Days at Belle Grove.
(National Trust)*

*Massanutten Mountain and the fields of the
Shenandoah Valley seen from the Belle Grove
doorway. (L.A. Durnier)*

series of pointed arches. Jefferson used these semicircular fans at several pavilions on the lawn of the University of Virginia. The Doric portico is another detail with which Jefferson invariably graced his houses. Even the layout, limited as it is to rectangular rooms, has the type of circulation he often used in his smaller houses. Belle Grove has a T-shaped hall similar to one Jefferson designed for Edgemont.

Belle Grove also reflects the different cultures of the valley settlers. Traces of the Germanic customs that Jost Hite brought with him to Virginia in 1732 can be seen in the house built by his grandson two generations later. The well-proportioned limestone exterior with its graceful roof and tall chimneys is a product of local materials and customs as well as the architectural modes of the period. Germanic details include the solidity of the stone foundations and the careful stonework of the sturdy walls.

Originally the house was built without the present portico and the west wing. Early records dated 1803 and 1805 describe Belle Grove as a "Stone Dwelling house 1 Story high, 74 by 40 feet covered with wood." The entrance door is emphasized with architectural trim, found on some other fine houses in the valley and characteristic of the Federal style.

The interior is distinguished by fine woodwork, much of it transitional between the Georgian and Federal periods. Other notable features include decorative mantelpieces, a Federal parlor and fanlights over the cross hall doorways (a rarity in the interiors of Virginia mansions).

In 1802, Eleanor Madison Hite died, leaving a young son and daughter. The following year, Hite married another Orange County woman, Ann Tunstall Maury, daughter of Rev. Walker Maury. The marriage produced 10 children born between 1805 and 1819, all of whom grew to adulthood. It was probably during this time that the wing and portico were added to Belle Grove.

By 1814, Issac Hite owned 7,437 acres in Frederick County and additional land in neighboring counties. Farming was his primary occupation; he was described as "an industrious and observant owner" who used the most advanced methods of farming.

After Hite died in 1836, his widow continued to operate the house and farm. Following her death in 1851, the property remained in the family until 1862, when Benjamin B. and John W. Cooley purchased the house and 619 surrounding acres.

Belle Grove was severely affected in the Civil War, primarily by the Battle of Cedar Creek on October 19, 1864. Active fighting had taken place in the Shenandoah Valley that fall, with

Main entrance to the house, with its delicate columned portico. (Marler Photo)

Dogs herding sheep at Farm Craft Days recall Belle Grove's farming heritage. (L.A. Durnier)

two battles during September. The larger Union Army had been unable to score a decisive victory. Confederate Gen. Jubal Early, encamped near Strasburg, recognized that any Confederate victory here would have to be a tactical one. At 5 a.m. he ordered an attack on the sleeping Union Army drawn up around Gen. Philip Sheridan's headquarters at Belle Grove. With the advantage of surprise, Early's troops seemingly scored a complete rout of the Northern troops.

It was late morning before Sheridan appeared on the scene. He had been in Washington conferring with Secretary of State Stanton, spent the night in Winchester and awakened to the sound of distant firing. When news of the battle reached him, Sheridan immediately rode to the front. By late afternoon, Union troops reversed the tide and the Shenandoah Valley remained firmly in Northern hands.

Following the Civil War, various families owned Belle Grove. In 1867, the Cooley family sold it to James Davison, an Englishman. Five years later, John Grant Rose from Edinburgh, Scotland, purchased the property and in 1881 sold it to J. Wilson Smellie. In 1907, Andrew Jackson Brumback acquired Belle Grove and in 1919 gave it to his son, J. Herbert Brumback, who operated the house as an inn.

In the late 1920s, Francis Welles Hunnewell of Wellesley, Mass., came to the Shenandoah Valley to collect botanical specimens. At this time, he was secretary to the Harvard Corporation and phaenogamic curator of the New England Botanical Club. Discovering in 1929 that Belle Grove was for sale, he purchased it from Brumback and engaged Washington architect Horace Peaslee to restore the house.

Hunnewell's foresight helped assure that Belle Grove's architectural integrity was maintained. Recognizing the historical and architectural importance of Belle Grove and expressing concern for its future care, Hunnewell bequeathed the house and 100 acres of farmland to the National Trust. On his death in 1964, the National Trust received the property and opened it to the public in 1967. Today, operated by Belle Grove, Inc., this National Historic Landmark is open as a historic house museum. By sponsoring numerous educational programs and special events such as Farm Craft Days, Belle Grove continues to play a significant role in preserving and promoting the life and culture of the Shenandoah Valley.

Belle Grove is located one mile south of Middletown, Va., on Route 11. It is accessible from the Middletown exit of Interstate 81, north of the Interstate 66 junction.

For more information, write: Executive Director, Belle Grove, Inc., P.O. Box 137, Middletown, Va. 22645.

Oatlands

A view of the mansion from its formal gardens.
(Marler Photo)

In 1798, Councillor Robert Carter of Nomini Hall gave approximately 3,500 acres in Virginia's Loudoun County to his son, George Carter, when he came of age. It was on this land, adjacent to Goose Creek near Leesburg, Va., that George Carter shortly after 1800 built the house later called Oatlands.

Materials essential to the construction of Oatlands house were available on the estate. Beginning in 1804, bricks for the mansion and its dependencies were molded and fired on the property. Wood was brought from the surrounding forests.

When Councillor Carter died in 1804, George Carter inherited and transferred some of the furnishings, books and family portraits from Nomini Hall to Oatlands. Carter continued the development of his estate, and by 1816 he had constructed a gristmill and a sawmill on the north bank of Goose Creek. The gristmill, which began operating in 1817, ground flour for President Monroe's nearby estate, Oak Hill, as well as for Oatlands and other Loudoun County farms. The area soon became the center of a thriving community that included the miller's residence, a blacksmith shop and a store.

In 1827, Carter added the prominent portico to the south facade. A volume from the extensive

Nomini Hall library, *A Treatise on Civil Architecture in which the Principles of That Art are Laid Down* by William Chambers (London, 1768) served as a reference for the owner in planning the addition. Letters from George Carter to his carver, sketches and specifications for the Corinthian capitals of the portico columns were tipped inside the book. (This copy of Chambers's treatise is still in the Oatlands library.) Henry Farnham of New York City executed the capitals, which were transported by ship to the port of Alexandria and by wagon to Oatlands. Carter also planned the formal terraced garden and planted many of the trees and boxwood that flourish on the estate today.

The plan of the house reveals a simple layout, but the wealth of decorative detail reflects originality and craftsmanship. The mansion has a central three-story section flanked by two-story wings and semioctagonal extensions. The exterior walls are stuccoed brick, painted a creamy buff color; the wood columns and trim are white. Noteworthy among the 13 rooms is an octagonal drawing room. Other notable features are staircases placed in each of the extensions, rather than traditional central stairs. The entrance hall reveals Adamesque (or Federal) design in the leaded tracery of the side windows and the fanlight over the door. A 19th-century chandelier hangs from an ornate medallion.

Detail of the hall chandelier and ceiling medallion. (Allen Studio)

A classically detailed doorway leads from the main hall to a breakfast room. (Marler Photo)

The entrance hall at Oatlands is distinguished by
a 19th-century chandelier and a Louis XV desk.
(Allen Studio)

In 1835, George Carter married a widow, Elizabeth Grayson Lewis. Two sons born of this marriage, George II and Benjamin, lived to adulthood.

In the 1830s, Carter made several changes in interior decoration reflecting the popularity of the Greek Revival style. Cornices and moldings were added to the drawing room and library, and an elaborate ceiling medallion was placed in the entrance hall.

The builder of Oatlands died in 1846 at the age of 69 and was buried in the Carter tomb in the Oatlands garden. His estate was inherited by his widow and two sons. With the advent of the Civil War, the Carters left Oatlands; George joined the Confederate Army, and Confederate troops were briefly billeted in the house. In 1863, having left the Army, George Carter II married Katherine Powell of Middleburg, Va., and returned to Oatlands.

The fortunes of the Carter family declined steadily after the war. Furnishings, family portraits and tracts of land were sold. In the 1880s and 1890s, the Carters opened their mansion to summer boarders. One of these was Phoebe Hearst, mother of William Randolph Hearst. Mrs. Hearst purchased the Carters' portrait of Councillor Carter (attributed to Sir Joshua Reynolds). Before the painting was shipped to San Simeon (the Hearst estate in California), however, the Carters had it copied. The copy, on loan from the family, is at Oatlands today.

In 1897, Oatlands was sold to Stilson Hutchins of Washington, D.C., founder of *The Washington Post*. Hutchins never occupied the house. Six years later, Mr. and Mrs. William Corcoran Eustis bought the estate. By this time, the mansion was in disrepair and the garden overgrown. The Eustis family intended to return Oatlands to its original beauty. Eustis was the grandson of William W. Corcoran, Washington banker and founder of the Corcoran Gallery of Art, and Mrs. Eustis was the daughter of Levi P. Morton, vice president under President Benjamin Harrison.

During the Eustis ownership, several changes were made to the mansion and the garden. A small porch was added at the rear of the house to give access from the octagonal drawing room to the boxwood grove. The garden was expanded—although it retained the basic design established by George Carter. Ruins of structures below the terrace were removed. A balustrade was built atop the retaining walls. A vegetable garden was transformed into a boxwood allee, with a reflecting pool at one end and a bowling green and gazebo at the other. Mrs. Eustis tended the boxwood planted by Carter and designed parterres and terraces with flowers and formal box borders. She also planted a number of specimen trees, including four *Magnolia grandiflora* in the garden.

Serving as the Eustises' country residence in summer and during the hunting season, Oatlands again flourished. Eustis, a distinguished sportsman who had hunted and won point-to-point races in England and Ireland (including the Meath Cup), was one of the founders of the Loudoun Hunt in 1894. He constructed the frame carriage house at Oatlands to provide stabling for the Eustis hunters and carriage horses and storage space for vehicles.

William Eustis died in 1921, but his widow continued to spend much of each year at Oatlands until her death in 1964. Their daughters, Mrs. David E. Finley and Mrs. Eustis Emmet, presented the 261-acre estate to the National Trust in 1965 in memory of their parents. Oatlands was designated a National Historic Landmark in 1972.

In 1974, an area of more than 900 acres encompassing several structures historically related to Oatlands was designated as Oatlands Historic District and placed in the National Register of Historic Places. This district includes Mountain Gap School, a late 19th-century one-room schoolhouse built on land set aside by George Carter in 1827; the Church of Our Savior, consecrated in 1878 and built on land deeded by the Carter family; and the Oatlands Mill site, which was donated to the National Trust in 1973 by Mr. and Mrs. Finley and Mrs. Emmet.

In 1979, Oatlands of the National Trust, Inc., assumed responsibility for the operation of the estate. The National Trust continues to own the property and assure its continued maintenance and preservation.

The Finley-Emmet lands adjacent to Oatlands are protected by open space easements held by the commonwealth of Virginia and the National Trust. These easements assure the future of the scenic vistas that surround the estate. Under Virginia's Open Space Land Act of 1966, sites in the Virginia Landmarks Register can be saved in perpetuity from destructive change to the natural environment.

The Oatlands visitor season opens each April 1 with Loudoun County Day. In early April, the Oatlands Equestrian Center is the scene of the point-to-point races of the Loudoun Hunt, which includes the William Corcoran Eustis Cup and other races.

Oatlands is six miles south of Leesburg, Va., on U.S. Route 15.

For more information, write: Executive Director, Oatlands, Route 2, Box 352, Leesburg, Va. 22075.

Drayton Hall

Majestically framed by live oaks, Drayton Hall is situated on the historic Ashley River near Charleston, S.C. Built between 1738 and 1742, it is the oldest and, according to many architectural historians, the finest surviving example of early Georgian architecture in the South. Because of its sophisticated design incorporating a two-story recessed Palladian portico, richly handcrafted interiors and dependencies (for which important archeological evidence exists), Drayton Hall is one of the most significant architectural sites in the U.S.

The Drayton family, which built and owned the mansion through seven generations, came to the American colonies in 1679. Like many of their neighbors, the Draytons moved from England to Barbados and finally to Charleston, the first permanent European settlement in Carolina. Thomas Drayton, the first of his family in the New World, settled along the Ashley River, the major transportation artery to the area's tidewater plantations, on land known today as Magnolia Gardens. When Drayton died, he left Magnolia to his eldest son and neighboring land to his youngest son, John.

In 1738, John Drayton, not yet 30, began construction of Drayton Hall, named for the family's ancestral seat in Northamptonshire,

Surviving war and weather, Drayton Hall stands today much as it did in the colonial South. (Carleton Knight III, National Trust)

*Drayton Hall entrance with its two-story recessed
Palladian portico. (Frances Benjamin Johnston,
Library of Congress)*

England. The architect of Drayton Hall has not been identified, but his sophisticated knowledge of existing architectural modes is apparent. He adhered closely to the English Palladian concept of design. The overmantel in the first-floor Great Hall is a close copy of one in Kent's *Designs of Inigo Jones* (1727). An example of the architect's sophistication is seen in the fact that the flanker buildings were set approximately two degrees off a line perpendicular to the main house. From a distance, the human eye corrects this offset—proving that the designer obviously knew how to use optical illusion to advantage. If the flankers had been placed perpendicular to the house, from a distance it would have appeared that they angled in toward the house.

From this estate, John Drayton supervised the operation of nearly a score of plantations throughout the region. These plantations produced the major cash crops (indigo, rice and cotton) that were brought to Drayton Hall and distributed from there.

During the American Revolution, the builder of Drayton Hall died. The estate passed to his son, his grandson and his great-grandson, all three named Charles and all three physicians. The fourth Charles Drayton, great-great-grandson of the builder, acquired Drayton Hall on the eve of the Civil War; because Charles was a minor, his uncle John managed the estate.

Detail of Drayton Hall's entrance hall doorway. (Frances Benjamin Johnston, Library of Congress)

A detail from the fireplace cornice in the
entrance hall. (Gale Alder)

An elaborate overmantel in the Ionic Room.
(James C. Massey)

The Civil War brought an end to the plantation system and with it the Drayton family fortunes. Unlike other plantation houses on the Ashley River, however, Drayton Hall was not destroyed when Union troops passed through Charleston. The Draytons had signaled that the house was being used for smallpox victims; whether this was ruse or fact, it worked, and the house was spared.

During and immediately after the war, the house occasionally was occupied by squatters and suffered from neglect. It was rescued from further deterioration in the late 1870s when a use was found for the large phosphate deposits on the land. The wealth accumulated during this period helped pay for much-needed repair, including replacement of the slate roof with tin and the covering of the brick pediment with imbricated wooden shingles. The two-story flanking dependency to the north, however, was destroyed by the earthquake of 1886 and the one to the south was razed in the 1880s after damage from a hurricane. The house has never had plumbing, gas lights, electricity or central heating.

By mid-20th century, the Drayton family stopped using the plantation house except for a few weeks in the spring and fall. Because of this declining use, they decided to seek out a new owner who could assure its continuing preservation. The Historic Charleston Foundation took the lead in this effort and in 1973 joined with the National Trust for Historic Preservation in a lease option to purchase the property from the owners, Charles H. and Frank B. Drayton and their children. By late 1974, funds for the purchase had been raised in a combined effort with the South Carolina Department of Parks, Recreation and Tourism, the National Park Service and the U.S. Bureau of Outdoor Recreation.

Today, the National Trust in conjunction with the state of South Carolina operates Drayton Hall as an unusual historic house museum. Surviving war and weather, this National Historic Landmark has not received any major restoration work, and only a few pieces of furniture have been placed in the house to provide a sense of scale for the large rooms. Rather than a full-scale restoration, the National Trust is attempting to impart to visitors architectural and scenic images of 18th-century America in an area where few comparable survivors remain.

Drayton Hall is located nine miles northwest of downtown Charleston on South Carolina Route 61 (Ashley River Road).

For more information, write: Administrator, Drayton Hall, Route 4, Box 276, Charleston, S.C. 29407.

The street side of The Shadows. (Gleason Photography)

The dining room looking out toward the rear loggia, which opens onto a garden sloping down to the Bayou Teche. (National Trust)

The Shadows-on-the-Teche

The Shadows-on-the-Teche, sited on the Bayou Teche in New Iberia, La., has been described as a house alive and mellow, like the lush vegetation of its surroundings. Built when many great houses were being constructed in the cane and cotton country, The Shadows is one of the major surviving examples of antebellum southern Louisiana architecture.

Wealthy planter David Weeks planned this town house in 1825 for his growing family. His wide holdings included Grand Cote on Weeks Island, Cypremort, Parc Perdu and Vermillion Bridge. As a seat to supervise his holdings, he chose a central location. He acquired four and one-half arpents—about four acres—of land in the town then known variously by its Indian name "Attakapas," its Spanish name "Nova Iberia" or simply "New Town."

In 1831 slaves started firing the distinctive pink bricks that were to be used in the mansion, while a steady flow of construction materials came from New Orleans and other cities. Although each detail of the building program was under David Weeks's constant direction—from the ordering of cypress timbers to the selection of paints and carpets—he entrusted the construction of the mansion to James Bedell, a master builder, and estate agent Boyd Smith. This owner-builder collaboration was a common practice in an era of few professional architects.

The completed mansion reflects both local interpretation of the prevailing Classical Revival style, with columns and other architectural elements in the Tuscan order, and the melange of foreign influences—Spanish, French and English—that culminated in the distinctive house styles of Louisiana. The exterior staircase, the second-story balustrades, absence of interior hallways and a first floor almost flush with the ground and paved with brick and marble are typical of many southern Louisiana country houses built before the Civil War. Cross ventilation, an important feature in the hot humid climate, is provided by the many opposing windows and doorways.

As the house neared completion in the spring of 1834, David Weeks sailed for New Haven, Conn., in a vain effort to recover his failing health. From there he sent furnishings to his wife for the new house—carpeting, mahogany and maple chairs, bureaus, washstands and Britannia oil lamps. In July, Mary Clara Conrad Weeks wrote her husband: "Think not that poverty has such horrors as you think. Your health is the worst we have to contend with. I would take a basket and pick cotton every day if it would do you any good!"

The pantry and workroom area of The Shadows.
(National Trust)

David Weeks died in New Haven in August, leaving to his widow the responsibility for managing the plantations and educating their six children.

Mrs. Weeks was an avid reader and gardener. A collection of books printed before 1865 is still at The Shadows along with a bookcase David Weeks sent her from New Haven. She cultivated an extensive garden and the live oaks she planted still grace the property.

In 1841 Mary Weeks married Judge John Moore, a Whig member of the U.S. House of Representatives. No children were born of this marriage, but the offspring of their previous marriages considered The Shadows their home.

The story of the family before the Civil War, and the bitter years that followed, is typical of the Louisiana planter class. It was a life tied to the rise and fall of the sugar and cotton markets. At its worst, it was a life of hard work, hurricanes and plagues of yellow fever, malaria and cholera; at its best, a colorful life with regular escapes to resorts from Virginia Springs and Newport to Niagara Falls and Saratoga.

The Civil War brought an end to this traditional plantation life. New Iberia became headquarters for Union generals Stephen G.J. Burnbridge and William B. Franklin during the Red River Campaign of 1864.

After the war, The Shadows faced continued

deterioration, although family fortunes improved somewhat in the 1870s with the development of the salt mine on Weeks Island.

When Weeks Hall, the great-grandson of The Shadows's builder, returned to his native Louisiana after service in World War I and art studies in Paris, he found the building and its dependencies drifting into ruin with a tangle of neglected gardens under the great oaks. He determined to return The Shadows to its former beauty and devoted the remaining years of his life to preserving the house and recreating the great garden around it.

In 1922 Weeks Hall engaged the firm of Armstrong and Koch, New Orleans architects, to undertake the restoration. Both Weeks Hall and Richard Koch, FAIA, kept detailed records of replacements and modern improvements.

Weeks Hall, described as "the last of the Southern gentlemen," also brought back, during the 1920s and 1930s, the gaiety and sparkle of antebellum hospitality. He was an intimate of many celebrities who were visitors at The Shadows, among them H.L. Mencken, W.C. Fields, Henry Miller, Max Ernst, Abe Rattner, Cecil B. de Mille, Lyle Saxon and Mae West. Weeks Hall kept their signatures on a prized door that still can be seen in the ground-floor office.

Henry Miller wrote of Weeks Hall in *The Air-Conditioned Nightmare,* "He was an artist to

Rosewood bed in a second-floor bedroom that was originally a sitting room. (National Trust)

One of the four statues of the seasons placed in the gardens at The Shadows by Weeks Hall during the 1922 restoration. (Katherine McAllister)

his fingertips. . . . He saw the relatedness of all things. . . . In a sense it might be said of him that he had already completed his great work. He had transformed the house and grounds, through his passion for creation, into one of the most distinctive pieces of art which America can boast of. He was living and breathing in his own masterpiece, not knowing it, not realizing the extent and sufficiency of it. . . . I felt his presence all through the house, flooding it like some powerful magic fluid. He had created that which in turn would recreate him." At the bequest of Weeks Hall the National Trust for Historic Preservation received The Shadows on his death in 1958.

In 1961, the National Trust restored The Shadows, based on the accounts of Weeks Hall and Richard Koch and on the thousands of family documents—many dating to the 18th century—in the Louisiana State University Library. Today, this National Historic Landmark is operated as a historic house museum, promoting the unique history and culture of the bayou through exhibits and special events.

The Shadows-on-the-Teche is located in New Iberia, La., at the intersection of Center Street and East Main Street.

For more information, write: Administrator, The Shadows-on-the-Teche, P.O. Box 254, New Iberia, La. 70560.

Wright Home & Studio

Frank Lloyd Wright's Home and Studio in Oak Park, Ill., is one of his most important buildings—historically and architecturally. Wright lived and worked here for more than 20 years, during the formative period of his career. It was here that he designed his first major buildings. And, using the Home and Studio as experimental models, it was here that he developed and perfected the Prairie style.

In 1887, at the age of 20, Wright moved from his family's home in Madison, Wis., to Chicago. Almost immediately, he began work as a draftsman and renderer for architect Joseph Silsbee. Two years later, Wright was draftsman for the firm of Adler and Sullivan.

Until this time, he had lived on Chicago's south side; however, in 1889, he married and wanted to build a home of his own. In May of that year, Wright purchased a lot in Oak Park, a sparsely developed suburb to the west of Chicago. Construction began in August and was completed within six months.

The house was basically of a Shingle-style design, similar to the work of Silsbee when Wright was his employee. Yet, in his first house design, Wright brought the picturesque irregularities of the style under his own particular geometric discipline. Every part has been simplified. A great triangular gable end rests directly on an undulating wall band containing windows and doors. This band sits, in turn, on a brick base that also forms a parapet wall for two half-round terraces that bulge out from the house.

The interior plan was a simple one: fireplace at the center, living room across the front of the house, dining room and kitchen across the back. Still, it suggests Wright's concern for interrelated spaces, the centrality of the fireplace in his house designs and the use of natural light. All the living spaces open onto one another through wide openings; only the kitchen is closed off with a swinging door. The fireplace in the center provides not only good radiant heat, but also a strong core to the home. The kitchen is sited so that it receives both eastern and southern light, which illuminates it naturally at the time when it is used most. Wide stairs lead to the upper rooms, with a large studio across the front of the house for Wright's drafting work and two bedrooms across the back separated by a bath.

Construction of the house was financed by a $5,000 loan from Louis Sullivan with the understanding that Wright would devote his full energies to the office and not accept outside commissions. However, between 1891 and 1893, Wright accepted independent commissions for

Side view of the building, showing the steeply
gabled house. (National Trust)

The dynamic massing and varied materials
reflect the numerous changes that Wright made
to his studio over the years. (National Trust)

nine houses, designing them at home in Oak Park. When Sullivan became aware of this outside work, he thought that it constituted a conflict of interest. Wright left to open his own office and devoted himself full time to independent practice.

By 1895, Wright's family had expanded to include four children. To accommodate this growth, he made a substantial addition to the house, designing a kitchen and maid's room on the ground floor and a barrel-vaulted playroom on the second. A dining room was created out of the former kitchen with the addition of a bay window.

In 1898, Wright added the studio building adjacent to the house and formally moved his practice from Chicago to Oak Park. The large studio consisted of a foyer, octagonal library, a private office, vault and a two-story drafting room with balcony.

In subsequent years, Wright's practice grew and included many of the most important works of his career, including the Robie House, Unity Temple and the Larkin Office Building. It was during this time that he hired and trained his best-known assistants: Walter Burley Griffin, Marion Mahoney, William Drummond, Francis Barry Byrne and John S. Van Bergen. Wright also increasingly used the house and studio buildings as an architectural laboratory, frequently changing and updating the design features in keeping with his new ideas about architecture.

In 1909, Wright closed the studio and took an extended trip to Europe to work on a major monograph of his work, to be published by Ernst Wasmuth in Berlin. The Oak Park days were over. Wright seemed to be seeking a new independence. His work in revolutionizing the design of the American house was complete in terms of his Prairie style.

Wright returned briefly to Oak Park in 1911. At that time, he made extensive changes to the house and studio so that the buildings could be rented as several living units to bring income to his wife, from whom he was now separated. In 1911, Wright built a new home and workplace in southern Wisconsin—the first Taliesin. Wright's first family continued to live in the converted studio until about 1918.

About 1925, the architect sold the Home and Studio. There were several owners in the next decades. The property was acquired by Mr. and Mrs. Clyde Nooker in the mid-1940s. During the Nookers' stewardship, excellent care was taken of the aging building. They recognized the importance of the property and accomplished the majority of restoration work visible today. In 1966, they opened the building for the first public tours. But the expense of maintenance was too much for two private individuals.

Barrel-vaulted playroom in the Wright home.
(Curt Teich and Company)

The Frank Lloyd Wright Home and Studio Foundation was founded in 1974 with the intent of acquiring, restoring and operating the building for public benefit. The group had negotiated the purchase for several years following the announced sale of the property. In May 1974, as an interim step, the Oak Park Development Corporation took title to the property, aided by a loan from Avenue Bank and Trust Company in Oak Park. A group of guides was quickly trained, and the building was opened to the public on a regular schedule.

The immediate goal of the foundation was to repay the original loans and assure public ownership. An agreement was reached with the National Trust for Historic Preservation whereby it agreed to pay one-half the acquisition costs, with the balance to be raised by the foundation. In the first years of operation, the foundation raised nearly $100,000 for this purpose. Under the terms of the agreement ratified in August 1975, the National Trust holds title to the property and leases it to the foundation at a nominal sum. The foundation retains the responsibility for operation, maintenance and restoration of the property.

Today, the foundation operates the Oak Park Tour Center, providing year-round guided tours of the Home and Studio and the Oak Park Historic District (which contains 25 Wright-designed structures, the largest collection in the world). It also sponsors public lectures, publication of research findings, acquisition of objects and the continued restoration of the Home and Studio.

This property presents a particularly complex restoration challenge because the Home and Studio was constantly changing under Wright's hand while he lived and worked there. The foundation interpreted the property as a compilation of Wright's evolving design attitudes. His residency was a period of continuing functional adjustments and aesthetic refinement to the buildings, from the experimental efforts of the 1890s through the mature Prairie style of the early 1900s. This continuum stopped with Wright's departure in 1909. Few of the subsequent changes contributed significantly to Wright's earlier expression and, in fact, obscured much of the original design and purpose. The foundation thus chose to focus on restoration to the 1909 date, at the peak of studio activity, while allowing for certain reasonable exceptions, including adaptive use for foundation activities.

The Frank Lloyd Wright Home and Studio is located at 951 Chicago Avenue, Oak Park.

For more information, write: Executive Director, Frank Lloyd Wright Home and Studio, 951 Chicago Avenue, Oak Park, Ill. 60302.

*A portion of the gardens at Filoli, with the
original coach house in the background. (Jack E.
Boucher, Historic American Buildings Survey)*

Filoli

A glimpse of quail and deer along a quiet country lane, magnificent oaks framing an imposing mansion of warm brick, well-manicured lawns and gravel paths inviting the visitor to gardens beyond—this is Filoli in Woodside, Calif.

The estate originally was part of a land grant to John Coppinger made in 1840 by the Mexican governor of Alta California. Known as "Rancho Canada de Raymundo," the land passed through several hands in the latter half of the 19th century until 1914, when William Bowers Bourn II purchased it.

Bourn, the son of one of California's wealthiest men, attended Cambridge University in England. It was his admiration for the British style of life and architecture that inspired him to create Filoli. The terrain reminded him of the Lakes of Killarney area in Ireland known as the Muckrose estate, which he had purchased in 1910.

To design the main residence, Bourn employed Willis Polk. Polk had designed several personal and business buildings for the family, including Bourn's San Francisco town house. Bourn chose the building site on a gentle rise amid a magnificent stand of live oak trees. Polk oriented the house parallel to the valley and placed it on a raised earth podium about four feet above the natural grade of the land.

The house is basically U-shaped with the main portion of the mansion at the bottom and aligned to the north-south axis of the valley. While the house is largely Georgian in style, Polk used other architectural traditions in the design. The arched window heads of the first floor, the exterior Flemish bond brick and the details of the trim are all from the Stuart period, while the tile roof is clearly in the Spanish tradition. The two-story house covers 18,000 square feet. The interior space is divided into 43 rooms excluding baths, closets and storage space. Noteworthy are the 17 white marble fireplaces, the white marble baths, parquet wood floors, impressive crystal chandeliers and massive murals.

The arrangement of the rooms is formal. A central hallway runs the full length of both floors of the main section of the house. On the ground floor, the main rooms are laid out along the valley side, with the dining room on the south end next to the living room. A large central reception hall is in the center. A library and study are to the north. On the east side of the central hallway are the entrance foyer, bathrooms and pantries. The northeast wing contains a ballroom, the southeast servant areas and the main kitchen. The main stairway is located off-center at the entrance to the ballroom in the northeast wing. On the second floor are 10 family bedrooms and eight baths on both sides of the central hallway.

Throughout the first floor and the main stairway, all interior doors are decorated with Corinthian pilasters, engaged columns and pediments of various styles. Entrances to the principal rooms have elaborate scrolled pediments; the interiors of these rooms are paneled in dark oak, with extensive molding and classical cornices. All exterior doors and windows on the first floor have the typical Georgian fanlight with this arch echoed in the barrel-vaulted ceiling of the main-floor hallway.

Contemporaneous with the design of the house, Bourn picked Bruce Porter to design the setting and gardens. Porter was then the leading landscape architect in San Francisco. Sixteen acres of formal gardens grace the south side of the estate, with the main central axis of the garden becoming a grand allee. The actual planting was supervised by Isabelle Worn.

In 1936, both William Bourn and his wife died. The estate was purchased by Mr. and Mrs. William P. Roth. Mrs. Roth not only preserved and renewed the original plantings, but also greatly enriched the garden with choice plant materials. Without altering Porter's bold design, she incorporated new and better strains of old

favorites. The garden is divided into a number of separate areas with microclimates that allow for a wide range of plantings. More than 200 Irish yews grace the garden, while several hundred-year-old Coast live oaks surround the house. Silvery-blue Atlas cedars shelter the entrance at the north end of the house.

Particularly impressive is the Chartres Cathedral Garden with its neat boxwood borders between the flower beds representing the lead outlines of stained-glass windows from the French cathedral. The design is copied from a two-story window, and an English holly hedge represents the masonry between the upper and lower windows. Colorful annuals and standard roses represent the stained glass.

In all seasons, the garden at Filoli has some point of beauty. The color scheme is enriched in the fall by Japanese maples and ginkgo trees. The dark green Irish yews form a rich background in winter when no leaves blur lines or curves and the pattern of the garden becomes clear. At this time, the many hollies bear their bright berries, including two spectacular Van Tol holly trees flanking the front portico of the house. Spring brings an explosion of color when the camellias, rhododendrons and magnolias burst into bloom. Along the drive facing the house and in the main courtyard are many species of magnolia including the beautiful

The main entrance to the house. (Jack E.
Boucher, Historic American Buildings Survey)

Tall trees provide a canopy over the Filoli garden.
(Jack E. Boucher, Historic American Buildings Survey)

Strybing White with its large white, dovelike blooms in the early spring. As the camellias, azaleas and rhododendrons reach their peak, the weeping Japanese cherry trees delight the visitor with their spectacular bloom. As the season changes, more than 500 roses of all colors begin their continuous display throughout the summer along with colorful annuals planted between boxwood borders.

In addition to her extensive care and maintenance of these 16 acres, Mrs. Roth also generously opened the house and gardens to botanical and horticultural societies. As a result, Filoli became world known and, in 1973, Mrs. Roth was awarded the Distinguished Service Medal of the Garden Club of America.

Mrs. Roth donated her estate and garden to the National Trust in 1975. The National Trust determined that a local nonprofit organization would be best suited to operate the property for public benefit. Filoli Center, Inc., was organized to lease the estate at a nominal fee. In this way, the property benefits from local administration and support while maintaining a close relationship with the National Trust. The actual operation of Filoli is further aided by a volunteer support organization, Friends of Filoli. The Friends give tours of the gardens, operate the garden shop and sponsor workshops, lectures and concerts. Each year the Friends also

undertake one or more benefit events to raise money for needed capital improvements and repairs. Together, this coalition of the National Trust, Filoli Center and the Friends of Filoli assures the continued preservation and active public utilization of this elegant house and garden.

Located 28 miles south of San Francisco and 3.7 miles northwest of Woodside, Filoli is accessible from Interstate 280 at the Edgewood Road exit.

For more information, write: Executive Director, Filoli Center, Canada Road, Woodside, Calif. 94062.

Colophon

This limited edition of "American Landmarks" is the ninth in a series of Christmas Keepsakes distributed to our many friends and employees of York Graphic Services, Inc., of York, Pennsylvania. It was produced and designed under the direction of Howard N. King and by members of our staff with the design expertise of C. Richard Witson, art director of Armstrong Cork Company, whose calligraphy adorn many of the pages. The type is 10 point Garamond Book Condensed, leaded 2-1/2 points. Four thousand copies have been printed and bound on Curtis Colophon Text White by the C. Ernst Bischoff Printing Company of York, Pennsylvania. All for the joy of doing.

Detail of the classical, pedimented entrance to Cliveden in Philadelphia. (Cortlandt Hubbard, Historic American Buildings Survey)